MW00787846

Annabel Lee

By Edgar Allan Poe

Edited and illustrated by Samantha Seebeck

It was many and many a year ago,
   In a kingdom by the sea,
That a maiden there lived whom you may know
   By the name of Annabel Lee;

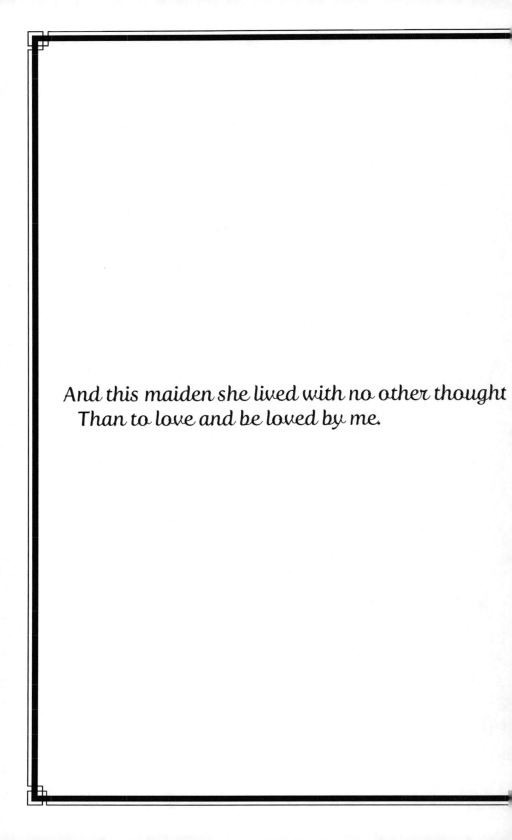

And this maiden she lived with no other thought
Than to love and be loved by me.

I was a child and *she* was a child,
In this kingdom by the sea,

But we loved with a love that was more than love—
   I and my Annabel Lee—
With a love that the wingèd seraphs of Heaven
   Coveted her and me.

And this was the reason that, long ago,
  In this kingdom by the sea,
A wind blew out of a cloud, chilling
  My beautiful Annabel Lee;

So that her highborn kinsmen came
And bore her away from me,

To shut her up in a sepulchre
In this kingdom by the sea.

The angels, not half so happy in Heaven,
Went envying her and me—

Yes!—that was the reason (as all men know,
In this kingdom by the sea)

That the wind came out of the cloud by night,
Chilling and killing my Annabel Lee.

But our love it was stronger by far than the love
   Of those who were older than we—
   Of many far wiser than we—

And neither the angels in Heaven above
Nor the demons down under the sea

Can ever dissever my soul from the soul
  Of the beautiful Annabel Lee;

For the moon never beams, without bringing
me dreams
   Of the beautiful Annabel Lee;

And the stars never rise,
but I feel the bright eyes
  Of the beautiful Annabel Lee;

And so, all the night-tide, I lie down by the side
  Of my darling—my darling—
ny life and my bride,

In her sepulchre there by the sea—
In her tomb by the sounding sea.

Made in the USA
Las Vegas, NV
11 December 2024

13882176R00021